Mystery Solvers

KEY QUEST

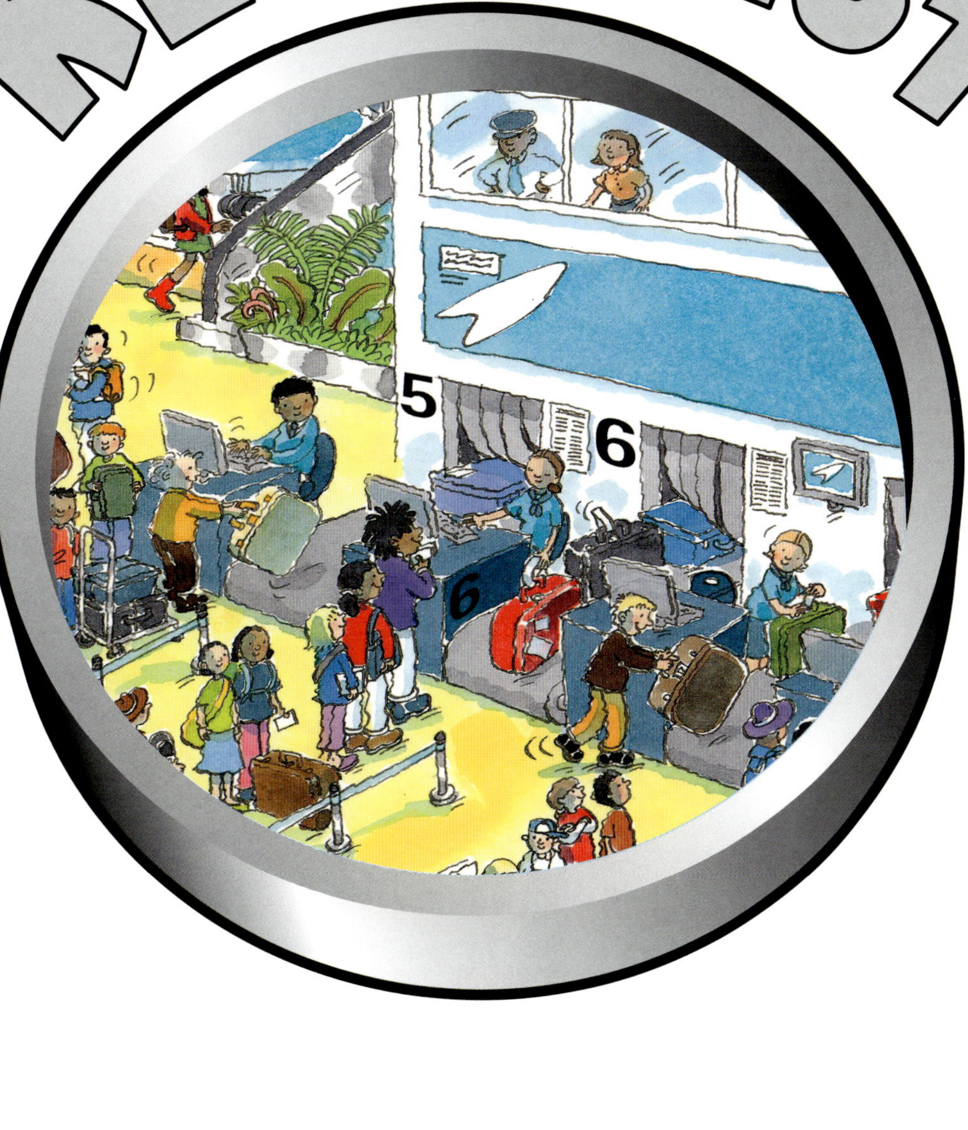

Parragon

Bath · New York · Singapore · Hong Kong · Cologne · Delhi · Melbourne

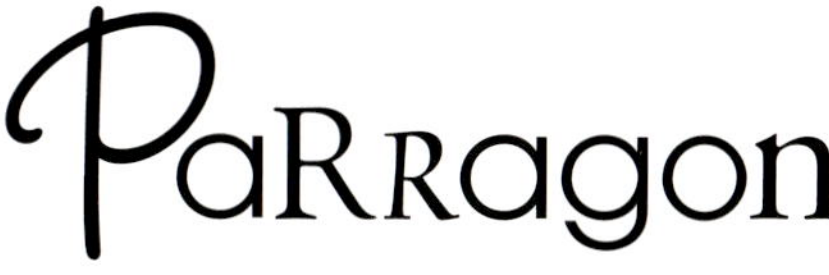

First published by Parragon in 2007

Parragon
Queen Street House
4 Queen Street
Bath BA1 1HE, UK

ISBN 978-1-4054-9541-7

Printed in China
Please retain this information for future reference.

MYSTERY SOLVER

MAGNIFY THE MYSTERY!

Dogs see, smell, and dig better than anyone. They make great detectives.

You can do it, too, by using your brains and your magnifying glass.

Good luck. **Woof!**

THE ANSWERS ARE AT THE BACK, BUT GOOD DETECTIVES DON'T LOOK UNTIL THE END.

MYSTERY MANSION!

SIMPSON TOLD TOM THAT HIS UNCLE WAS A FAMOUS EXPLORER AND THAT HE LOVED PUZZLES AND COLLECTING MINIATURE THINGS.

Your uncle asked me to give you this letter and a magnifying glass, Sir.

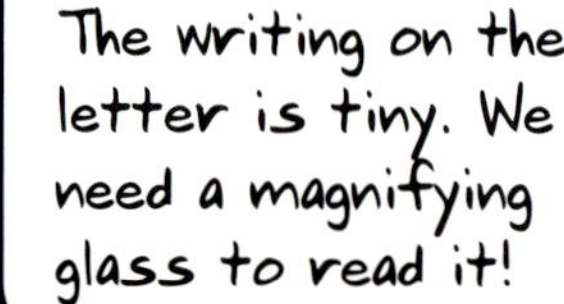

Use your magnifying glass to read the letter from Uncle George.

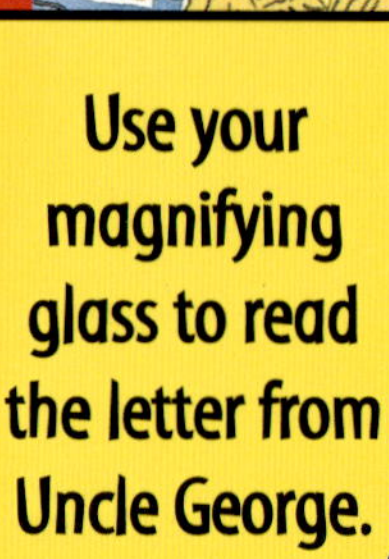

Dear Tom,

Welcome to Mystery Mansion. It is not all it seems. To find its key you must show yourself worthy by solving its clues. They will take you on a long journey, but if you prove fit for the task, you will get a great reward.

You must start by finding nine clues that you will need for your journey. You will find them in and around Mystery Mansion. Good luck!

Ask Simpson if you need anything.

Uncle George

Uncle George

Can you find Uncle George's mini treasures hidden in the house?
A tiny model of a house.
A tiny model of a bear.
A tiny shoe.
A painting.
The clues are inside folded pieces of paper. Help Tom and Buster find five folded pieces of paper hidden in Mystery Mansion.
Use your magnifying glass here to find out what else Buster is searching for.
Buster can smell some mice. Can you find six little mice scurrying around the mansion?

SECRET GARDEN!
The search for the rest of the clues continued in the garden of Mystery Mansion.
We've still got four more clues to find. But where do we start?
May I suggest you look in your uncle's garden, Sir?
Help Tom and Buster find the last four folded pieces of paper that Uncle George left for Tom hidden in the garden.

Uncle George kept some of his mini treasures in the garden. Can you find them all?
A model of a boat.
A garden gnome.
A tiny wheelbarrow.
A model of a dragon.
Buster has found some rats in the garden. Can you find all six rats?

AIRPORT ARRIVAL!

Follow Uncle George's directions to help Tom and Buster find the important number hidden at the airport.

CLUE ONE

Dear Tom,

Here are my directions to locate the important number you need:

1) Start by the green door handle.
2) Go past the blue arrow.
3) Turn right at the red circle.
4) Turn right at the sign of the car.
5) Turn left at the sign of the boat.

You will find the number you need in front of you.

Best wishes,

Uncle George

Uncle George

PS: I have hidden a small gold plane at the airport. Can you find it?

Keep a note of the important numbers you discover as you work through this book. You'll need them later!

Buster has seen six cockroaches in the airport. Can you help him find them all?

FIND IT IN THE FOREST!

The next clue took Tom and Buster to Canada.

THE CLUE TOLD TOM AND BUSTER TO SEARCH THE FOREST FOR THE NEXT IMPORTANT NUMBER.

Follow Uncle George's directions to help Tom and Buster find the important number hidden in the forest.

CLUE TWO

Dear Tom,

Here are my directions to locate the important number you need:

1) Start at the campsite.
2) Turn left near the black tree.
3) Turn left at the sign of the bee.
4) Turn right at the heart.
5) Turn left past the sign of the bear.

You will find the number you need on the second cave on the right.

Best wishes,

Uncle George

Uncle George

PS: I have hidden a gold apple in the forest. Can you find it?

Buster has seen some rabbits living in the forest. Can you help him find six rabbits?

MOUNTAIN HIGH!

Follow Uncle George's directions to help Tom and Buster find the important number hidden in the Alps.

The next clue led Tom and Buster to the snowy slopes of the European Alps.

ONCE THEY ARRIVED, THEY GOT READY TO SEARCH FOR THE NEXT IMPORTANT NUMBER.

Are you ready to search for more clues, Buster?

Ready as I'll ever be.

CLUE THREE

Dear Tom,

Here are my directions to locate the important number you need:

1) Start by the blue horse.
2) Turn right by the green circle.
3) Turn left by the purple flower.
4) Turn right by the red arrow.
5) Take the ski lift with the square symbol to the top.

You will find the number you need in the third window on the left.

Best wishes,

Uncle George

PS: I have hidden a silver bird in the Alps. Can you find it?

Buster has found hamster like creatures called marmots living on the mountain. Can you find six of them?

CANYON CRAZY!

Follow Uncle George's directions to help Tom and Buster find an important number hidden in the canyon.

CLUE FOUR
Dear Tom,
Here are my directions to locate the important number you need:
1) Start by the fir tree path.
2) Turn left by the black arrow.
3) Walk over the stones.
4) Go straight ahead at the sign of the sun.
5) Turn left up the steps.
You will find the number you need on the second boulder on the left.
Best wishes,
Uncle George
PS: I have hidden a little gold goat model in the canyon. Can you find it?
Buster has found some snakes in the canyon. See if you can find six of them.

VACATION ISLAND!

Follow Uncle George's directions to help Tom and Buster find an important number hidden on the vacation island.

CLUE FIVE

Dear Tom,

Here are my directions to locate the important number you need:

1) Start by the boat sign.
2) Turn right by the blue circle.
3) Turn left by the red sign.
4) Turn right past the two barns.
5) Cross the bridge.

Look up to find the number you need.

Best wishes,

Uncle George

Uncle George

PS: I have hidden a gold fish on the island. Can you find it?

Buster can smell some stray cats living on the island. Can you help him find six cats?

THEME PARK RIDE!

The next clue took Tom and Buster to a world-famous theme park.

Uncle George is certainly sending us on a long trip.

Follow Uncle George's directions to help Tom and Buster find an important number hidden in the theme park.

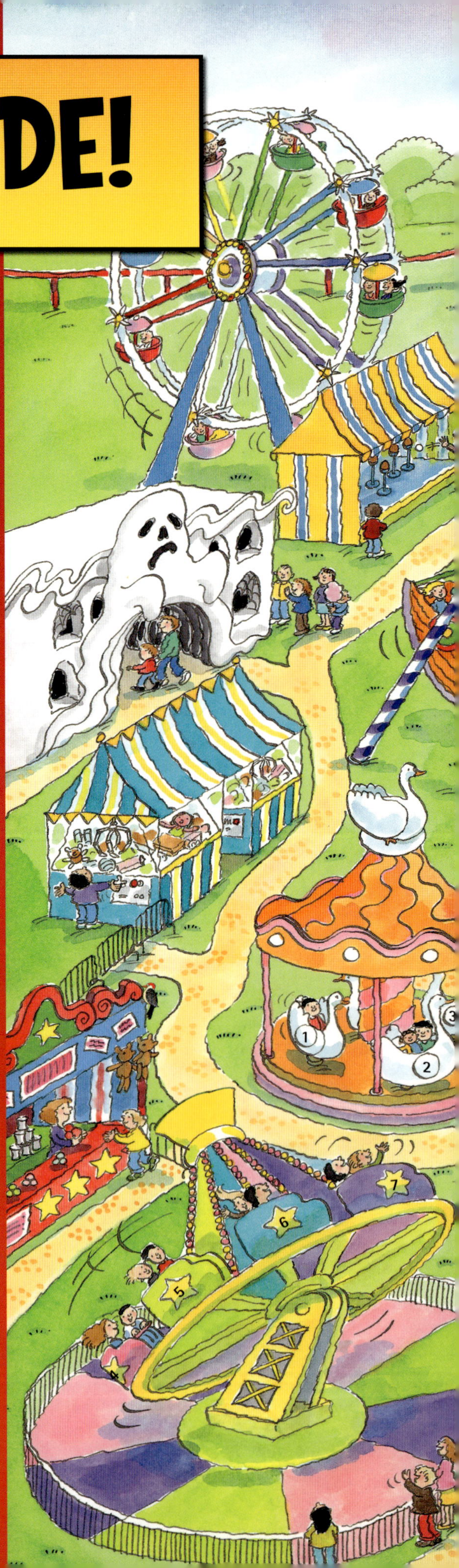

CLUE SIX

Dear Tom,

Here are my directions to locate the important number you need:

1) Start by the big clown face.
2) Turn right at the swans.
3) Turn right at the ghost.
4) Go past the rocket.
5) Stop to get a drink.

You will find the number you need above you.

Best wishes,

Uncle George

PS: I have hidden a gold crown in the theme park. Can you find it?

PPS: Keep going, it will be worth it!

Buster can smell woodpeckers living in the theme park. Can you help him find six of them?

THE BIG CITY!

The next clue sent Tom and Buster on their travels once again to a big city.

BUSTER BARKED TO CALL SOME OF THE CITY DOGS. SEVERAL TURNED UP TO HELP WITH THE SEARCH.

Follow Uncle George's directions to help Tom and Buster find an important number hidden in the city.

CLUE SEVEN

Dear Tom,

Here are my directions to locate the important number you need:

1) Start by the red door handle.
2) Turn left by the shooting star.
3) Turn right after the green building.
4) Turn right again.
5) Go past the man on a horse and walk underneath the passageway.
6) Cross over the street and turn left.
7) Stand at the blue bus.

You will find the number you need above your head.

Best wishes,

Uncle George

Uncle George

PS: I have hidden a gold wheelbarrow

Buster has sniffed out little lizards living in the nooks and crannies of the city. Can you find all six of them?

PORT PUZZLE!

Follow Uncle George's directions to help Tom and Buster find an important number hidden in the port.

CLUE EIGHT

Dear Tom,

Here are my directions to locate the important number you need:

1) Start at the gate.

2) Turn right at the number 21.

3) Turn left at the number 4.

4) Turn left by the number 10.

5) Turn right by the number 1.

You will find the number you need in front of you.

Best wishes,

Uncle George

Uncle George

PS: I have hidden a rare gold bird around the port. Can you find it?

Buster has found some more rats living around this port. Can you find six of them?

ANCIENT ANSWERS!

The last clue took Tom and Buster to a famous historical ruin.

Follow Uncle George's directions to help Tom and Buster find an important number hidden in the ruins.

CLUE NINE

Dear Tom,

Here are my directions to locate the important number you need:

1) Start at the entrance marked with a cat and turn right.

2) Turn left by the fallen pillar.

3) Turn right by the tiny hand.

4) Turn left by the big vase.

5) Turn right at the steps.

You will find the number you need in front of you.

Best wishes,

Uncle George

Uncle George

PS: I have hidden a precious ruby ring around the ruins. Can you find it?

PPS: Well done! It's time to go home to Mystery Mansion.

Buster can see some snakes living around the ruins. Can you find six of them?

HOME SWEET HOME!

At last, Tom, Buster, and Simpson, the butler, made it back to Mystery Mansion with the nine important numbers.

SIMPSON GAVE TOM A MAP. IT WAS A LAYOUT OF THE MANSION.

Use the numbers on the map to work out a path through the mansion to an important door and a secret surprise.

On the way, you must search for a small key.

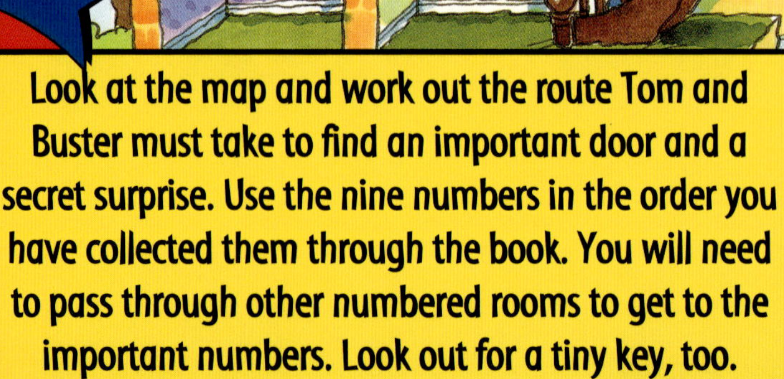

Look at the map and work out the route Tom and Buster must take to find an important door and a secret surprise. Use the nine numbers in the order you have collected them through the book. You will need to pass through other numbered rooms to get to the important numbers. Look out for a tiny key, too.

Inside, there are enough valuable miniature treasures to make Tom very rich, along with a note from Uncle George. Use your magnifying glass to read it.

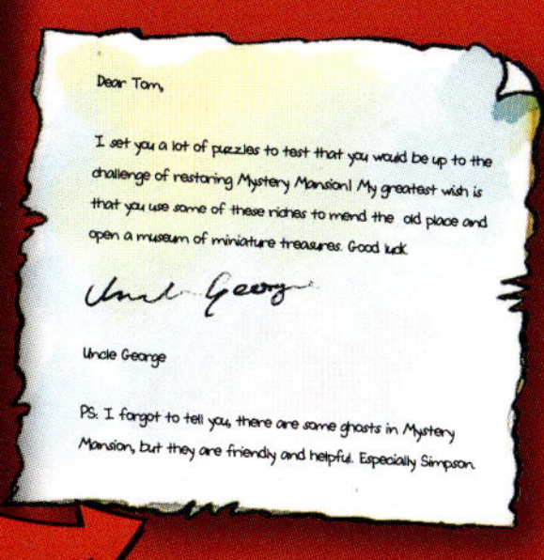
Dear Tom,

I set you a lot of puzzles to test that you would be up to the challenge of restoring Mystery Mansion! My greatest wish is that you use some of these riches to mend the old place and open a museum of miniature treasures. Good luck.

Uncle George

PS. I forgot to tell you, there are some ghosts in Mystery Mansion, but they are friendly and helpful. Especially Simpson.

Now Buster knows there are ghosts in Mystery Mansion, he wants to find all six of them. Can you help him?

ANSWERS

Pages 4–5

- Uncle George's mini treasures (red circle)
- Clues (purple circle)
- Buster's mini finds (blue circle)

Pages 6–7

- Uncle George's mini treasures (red circle)
- Clues (purple circle)
- Buster's mini finds (blue circle)

Pages 8–9

 Route taken

- Important number (red circle)
- Gold plane (purple circle)
- Buster's mini finds (blue circle)

Pages 10–11

Route taken

Important number

Gold apple

Buster's mini finds

Pages 12–13

Route taken

Important number

Silver bird

Buster's mini finds

Pages 14–15

Route taken

Important number

Gold goat

Buster's mini finds

ANSWERS

Pages 16–17

Route taken

Important number

Goldfish

Buster's mini finds

Pages 18–19

Route taken

Important number

Gold crown

Buster's mini finds

Pages 20–21

Route taken

Important number

Gold wheelbarrow

Buster's mini finds

Pages 22–23

Route taken

Important number

Gold bird

Buster's mini finds

Pages 24–25

Route taken

Important number

Ruby ring

Buster's mini finds

Pages 26–27

Important door

Secret surprise

Small key

Buster's mini finds

Turn to page 32 to find the path Tom and Buster took to find the important door and the secret surprise.

ANSWERS

Pages 26–27

— Route taken

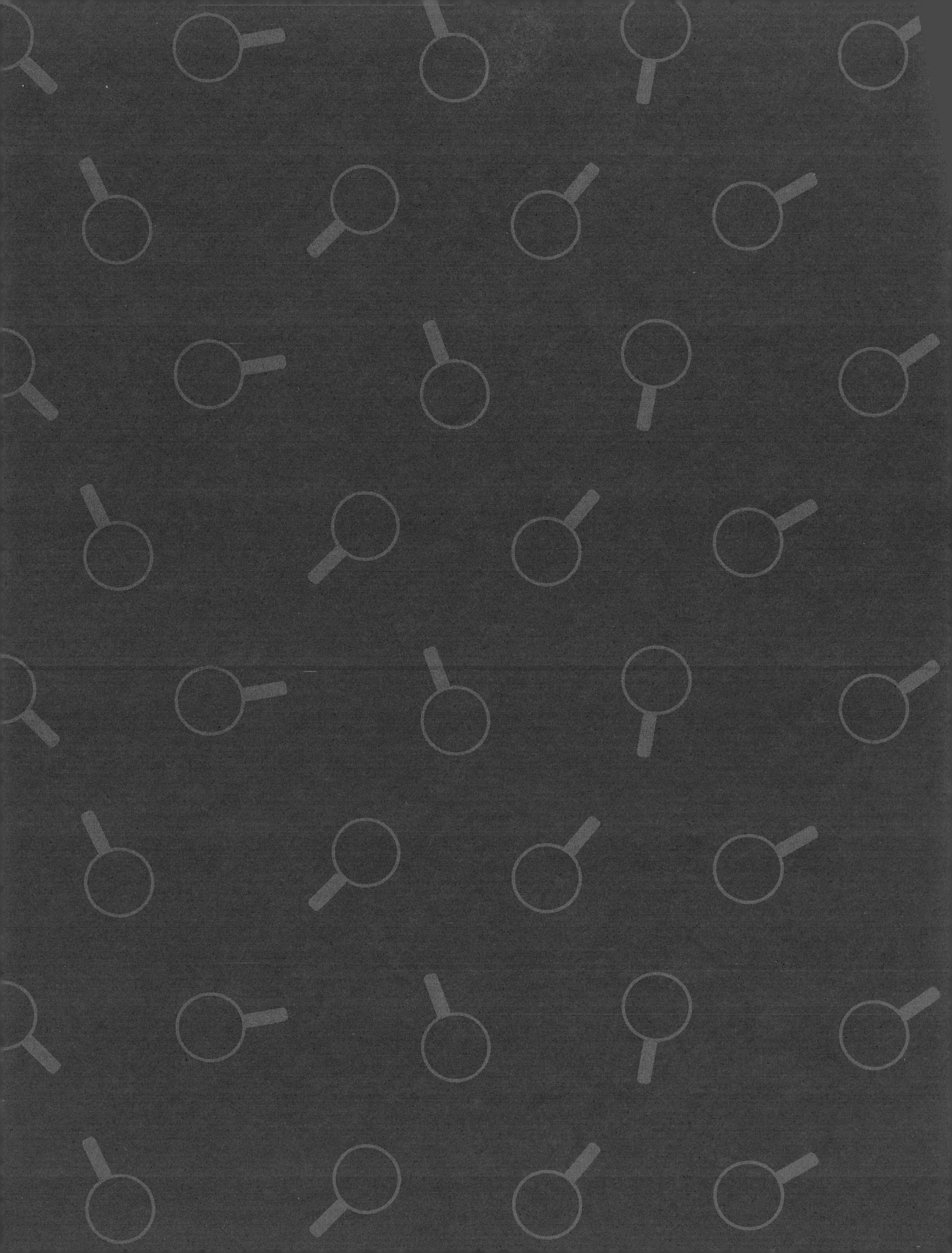